Intro to Shopify

A Beginner's Guide to Get You Going

By Reba Jones

Contents

Introduction

Are you considering starting a business? Do you want a brick and mortar store, or an online retail site? Do you want to have the physical ad space so that people literally stumble into your store, or do you want access to millions of buyers in an instant? What is a good platform to use for your business management? The following book should serve as a handy guide to getting your business off the ground. This guide will help your business tower over the competition. Full of tips and tricks, the following book should make for an interesting and informative read.

Note: This book assumes you have all the proper licensing in your state or country to start a business. This book assumes no responsibilities for any failure to comply with laws in your region, nor does this book intend to claim to know how to make your business successful. The following is simply advice and assumes no responsibility for any financial hardship caused by the following.

Shopify is one of the best options to meet the needs of your blossoming business. There are several reasons I espouse this opinion, but I shall not lay them out here. They will be laid out through the rest of the book.

I will let you know this up front, Shopify is one of the most affordable options, considering all that it offers. Plans start at nine USD ($) per month for their POS (point of sale) system and features, raising in cost when you add additional features. The details of these plans will be outlined in chapter one. Additionally, Shopify currently grants all users a fourteen-day free trial, to determine if you want to use their services before you pay for them.

Now that I have your attention, I shall explain the contents of each chapter. Every piece of information in this book was carefully selected out of the mounds of information available by me to help you and your business. As such, this carefully constructed piece should be read front to back, in order of writing. Skimming or skipping sections could easily mean you miss a piece of information that could be vital to the success of your business. Remember, planning is important, and this book will help you do that, and more.

Chapter one will help you set up your account with Shopify, giving you a basic tutorial of its features and layout, as well as granting you a checklist of what to do before you open your Shopify store to the public.

Chapter two will be all about determining what products to sell and how to find potential products, as well as how to acquire said products once found. Also, always make sure you have permission to sell other's work(s), especially for things that fall under intellectual property!

Chapter three will be about inventory management, how to stay on top of your inventory, when to reorder, and rough guidelines for how much to reorder.

Chapter four is about pinpointing your target demographic, finding people within that demographic, and explaining how to bring them into your store.

Chapter five is all about ways to keep your recently acquired customers coming back for more, an important skill for any successful business.

Chapter six speaks of how to compete with other companies and stay ahead of the pack. This chapter is your guide for dealing with competitors and adapting your business to meet the threats they bring to the table. This is required to keep someone from knocking you out of the game permanently.

Chapter seven is your guide to finding new products for your line up, once you have reached a point with your business where you are no longer looking to stay into the green, but how to maximize your profits. This chapter also covers how bringing on new products may impact your existing business.

In chapter eight, we will discuss making your business grow, from adding more physical locations, to when to add products, when to terminate products, and some non-traditional ways to spread awareness.

Chapter nine discusses the logistics of advertising your business and gives a few handy pointers on the dos and donts of advertising.

The tenth and final chapter will shed light on reinvesting. More specifically, how reinvesting a portion of your profits into your store can benefit your store in the long run.

Chapter 1: Starting Your Shopify Store

The first step to setting up your store on Shopify is to consider how you want to run your business. Do you want the business only to be an online store, or do you intend to set up traditional "brick and mortar" stores? Do you want Shopify to be your online market, or do you intend to use other sites such as Amazon, Facebook Marketplace, eBay, and/or even Craigslist? On the Shopify website, these additional avenues are listed as "sales channels." Once you have determined the number and type of sales channels you wish to operate, you are ready to choose a Shopify plan.

Choosing a Plan

Shopify offers a fourteen-day free trial so that you may sample their services; this plan will not sustain your business for long, so determining the pricing plan that is right for your business is a must. All Shopify plans offer a Point of Sale System (henceforth known as a POS system) for your use, but each price tier has more features than the last.

Every pricing plan includes a core set of features, these features include;

- Being able to sell any number of products

- Being able to use Shopify POS which allows for

      i. Managing inventory

      ii. Accepting payments through credit cards, debit cards, Apple Pay, and even Google Pay

- Access to the 24/7 Shopify POS technical support line

- An automatically generated, real-time (updated minutely) finances report, which covers sales, payments, liabilities, gift cards, and total sales

These features will henceforth be referred to as the "Shopify POS Core."

There are also features that all Shopify plans with a digital store (plans that begin at $29.99/month) include. These features include the following:

- Unlimited bandwidth and storage (meaning you will not be charged extra based on the number of orders, views, or customers your site gets)

- Being able to add unlimited pictures of your products (to ensure the customers are getting what they pay for and minimize returns)

- Support for third-party POS mobile and desktop applications

- Fraud Analysis (to ensure that you are being paid)

- A dedicated online store for your business

- In-app discount code generation (to encourage your loyal customers)

- Free SSL certificates (encryption so that your costumers can feel secure entering their payment information)

- Abandoned Cart Recovery (if a customer begins to check-out and enters their contact information but does not complete the order an automatic email will be sent to remind them that they still have items in their cart)

- The ability to print shipping labels from inside the application

- The ability to add multiple sales channels to your online store (such as Amazon and Facebook as well as a "buy button" that you can place on other websites)

These features will henceforth be known as the "Shopify Online Core." Listed below are the different Shopify Plans, as well as a brief description of them.

"Shopify Lite"- $9/month

This is the cheapest plan Shopify offers. Coming in at a price of $9 USD per month, it only offers the Shopify POS Core Features and the copiable "buy button."

Note: This plan does **NOT** have an online store component; it is meant only as support for a retail location.

"Basic Shopify"- $29/month

This plan costs $29 USD monthly, and in addition to the Shopify POS core features, this plan is the cheapest available plan to include the Shopify Online Core features. Additionally, this plan allows for two separate staff accounts, and up to a 64% percent shipping discount. The credit card fees for this plan are 2.9% + $0.30 for your online store, and 2.7% for your retail locations. Additionally, this plan allows you to access customer behavior reports, acquisition reports, and a marketing report for your online store.

"Shopify Plan"- $79/month

According to their website, this is Shopify's most popular plan, totaling in at $79 USD per month; this includes the Shopify POS Core Features, Shopify Online Core Features, and several others. This plan allows for up to five separate employee accounts for the back end of your business, unlimited Shopify POS staff PINs, the ability to use Shopify POS to register shifts, gift card creation, USPS Priority Mail Cubic pricing, more detailed reports, lower shipping rates, and lower card fees. The maximum shipping discount jumps 8%, making it 72%, while the online credit card rate drops to 2.6% + $0.30, while the in-person credit card fee drops to 2.5%. The additional reports include sales tax reports, and reports on customer behaviors (such as first time vs. returning customers, and customers by country)

Advanced Shopify- $299/month

This is the best plan Shopify has to offer, totaling $299 USD per month. In addition to the Shopify POS Core Features and the Shopify Online Core Features, and those included in the "Shopify Plan", this plan offers shipping rates calculated by a third party (allowing you to show the rates at checkout and giving precise rates), as well as further discounting the shipping rates, up to a 74% discount. It goes even further, allowing up to 15 staff accounts, and pushing the card fees down even more. The Credit card fee for an in-person sale is only 2.4%, and the fee for an online sale drops to only 2.4%+ $0.30 USD. This plan also allows for custom report generation.

Setting Up

Before beginning to set up products and inventory, you need to input some information about your store. Log in and temporarily password protect your store; this protection allows for testing and troubleshooting to be done before you go public. Then, fill out the basic information for your store. Name your store; choose your store's legal business name and address; add your billing information; set the defaults for currency and weight; set up the domain; set up staff members as necessary.

Testing and Troubleshooting

To make sure everything will run smoothly, add a couple of test orders, and test the following things:

- Successful and failed transactions
- Canceling orders

- Refunds
- Completing or partially filling orders
- Archiving your successful transactions

After everything is in working order, it is time to remove the site password and launch your store to the public. Remember that you can always re-password protect your site if you need to troubleshoot should something break.

Other Sales Channels

You may recall earlier when I mentioned sales channels offered with any Shopify plan. These are all highly recommended as they present your store to wider audiences.

If you have a personal website or blog, you may add a Buy Button for some of your most popular products with a link to your Shopify store.

You can also use other sites like Pinterest, Facebook, Etsy, Amazon, or even Facebook Messenger.

Shopify How To's

In order for the rest of the advice contained in the following pages to be clear, you must first understand many of the features of Shopify. The following section will explain these features clearly.

The image above is your home page. On the left side of the page, you will see the menu items, and at the center, you will see your name displayed above an interface. In addition to the menus on the left side, you will see the name of your store displayed. Before we address the menu items on the left, we will discuss the introductory tabs in the center of the home page. These tabs are meant to allow you to get the basics out of the way immediately. As such, they allow you to quickly add your domain and theme, as well as a button to take you to the page where you will add your first product. Next, I will explain how to add a product without this handy tab there, because it shall eventually be replaced with analytics for your store.

Adding a Product

In the left menu, notice the tab titled "Products." This tab will have an icon of a price tag. Click the tab. After you click the tab, the page it takes you to should look like this;

Click the blue "Add product" button to add your first product. After you add your first product, the button to create additional products will be moved to the top right-hand corner of this page. This is where you will create all of your products.

After you click the blue "Add product button," it will navigate you to the product information page. On this page, you will see multiple boxes containing space for all of the information about the product you wish to list. All of the basic information, such as product name, price, images, description, shipping weight, and variants will be input on this page. Additionally, there is an inventory section, in which you may enter your inventory information for the item if you wish for Shopify to handle your inventory tracking. If you opt for Shopify to track your inventory for you, it can automatically de-list an item from your website if you have run out, or you can tick the box that says "Allow customers to purchase this product when it is out of stock," and any customer who wishes to purchase it can, regardless of the stock status of the item. If you are having Shopify manage your inventory, then you will need to input a few more pieces of information. Firstly, the unit by which you are tracking your stock, (i.e., your stock keeping unit or SKU) you will need to input the barcode number, identifying different systems for your stocking system. Typical Barcode types are ISBN, UPC, and GTIN. There are other systems available.

Under this box is a box titled "Shipping." If you are selling a physical item, then you should leave the box titled "This is a physical product," checked. Otherwise, unlike the box and skip this section. For physical products, you will need to enter the approximate weight of your final, packaged item. This information is vital in calculating your shipping costs. If you intend to do international sales and shipping, you will need to fill out the Customs information boxes below the weight, under the header titled "Customs information." If you do not intend to sell and ship internationally, then you needn't bother filling out this section.

This final box on this page is titled "Variants" and is intended if there are different versions of this product available. If you would like to add a variant, click the blue "Add variant" button in the top right of this box. Upon doing that, two more boxes will appear inside this box. One of these boxes will be a place for you to put the name of the trait that can vary (i.e., size, color, fabric, etc.) and the other box will have a place for you to type the options your customers have to choose from.

There is a series of boxes on the upper right-hand side of your store that contains boxes for you to fill out additional information. Firstly, one of these boxes contains information on which sales channels you want this product to be available through. Then the block of boxes titled "Organization" allows you to create filters for your website based on product type, vendor, collections, or even product tags.

In the bottom right-hand corner of this page, you will find two buttons. They will be white and blue, and labeled "Cancel" and "Save product," respectively. Make sure you hit the "Save product" button before navigating away from the page!

To edit an item, simply navigate to the "Products" page and click on the name of the product you wish to edit. This should bring you to that product's information page. Once you are on this page, you will notice a few differences. Firstly, if you are returning to the product instead of the white "Cancel" button is on the right-hand side, you will find a red button labeled "Delete" on the left-hand bottom corner. There will also be some other options upon returning to a previously created product. In the top left of the page, there will be two additional buttons. One labeled "Duplicate," which creates a new product page exactly like the current one, and one that is labeled "Promote." From the promote tab, you can add ways Shopify can drive business to your store.

Managing Orders

Before you can manage and except product orders, you need to select a Shopify payment plan. There is a banner at the bottom of the screen saying how many days you have left in your free trial. In addition to giving you a count down on your trial, there is a blue "Select a plan" button on that banner. This is what you will use to select your payment play for Shopify. For more details on the plan options and features, see the beginning of this chapter.

Once you have selected a payment plan, you use the page labeled "orders" in the navigation pane with the drop box icon to track the status of orders, archive successfully completed orders, as well as viewing your abandoned cart recovery services and settings. It is from this page that you can send personalized emails to those who have items left in their cart, or people who began but did not finish the check-out process. You can also send these people personal discounts on their cart, to encourage them to place their order.

Customers

In the middle of the tab list on the navigation pane, you will find a tab marked "Customers," represented by a plan silhouette of an avatar. This tab is where the information about the customers who completed orders will be held. This is where you will find the customer's name, mailing address, email, and other contact information if they have provided it. In addition to automatically generated customer profiles, you can add manual profiles by clicking the blue "Add customer" button on the left-hand side of your screen.

In your store, you can choose to require customers to have an account, make them optional, or even disable them altogether. However, if customer accounts are enabled, a customer who makes a purchase while logged in will receive a smoother check out experience. This happens by auto-filling previously registered details for them in the shipping and payment information boxes, which they can view and change or simply move forward once they have verified that the information is correct. This feature must be enabled by you to function properly. The options to enable this feature can be founded in the "Settings" menu, under "Checkout" options, with the shopping cart icon.

Analytics

The analytics tab, indicated with a bar graph icon, is where you can find the statistics for your store, customer habit reports, and any other analytics Shopify compiles for you. There are two tabs within this page, which will be covered below.

In the tab labeled "Dashboards," you will find many boxes containing individual graphs and simplified data reports for your most commonly referenced metrics. These data panes include "Total sales," (organized by date and time), Your most frequently purchased products (measured by the number of units sold), the average order value for your store, sales by POS location, total orders over time, and sales by staff accounts. Below are some of the potential uses for each of the metrics.

For the "total sales over time" and "total orders" sections, which are organized by time and date, can be used to determine when you should run sales or perhaps a "happy hour" to entice more purchases. These metrics also allow you to see how these deals and any sales work for you. There is another report that contains the average order value for each time and day, which can help you make some critical decisions, such as when to run sales to reward your high-spending customers.

To view the full report of any of these metrics, there will be a blue "View report" link in the top right of each data box. When you click this link, it will take you to a more detailed report for that graph specifically. On this page, you will see options to print, export, and save your graph under a specific name and location to your device. These reports will contain larger graphs with more specific data and views that you can manipulate (such as changing the date range, grouping purchases by the hour, or take away grouping to reveal individual orders.)

Below these graphs will sit text-summaries of the data and information provided. Once again, you can change the specific details covered in the summary by manipulating the graph or by changing filters in the summary report options. You can also rearrange the data based on the columns given attribute. There are many potential column types, but the most prominent are covered below.

For the "Sales Over Time" report, the default columns are "hour" (which is pretty self-explanatory), "orders" (the number of orders placed), "gross sales" (the monetary value of all sales before any deductions are taken into account), "discounts" (any discounts the customer received), "returns" (how much money was lost in returns), "net sales" (the gross sales minus the amount of returns and discounts; how much you made before tax), "shipping" (money made through shipping costs), "taxes" (the amount of sales tax received), and "total sales" (the amount of money earned after taking everything into consideration). You can get to this report by clicking on the link in the "Total Orders" graph or the "Total Sales" graph.

Additional columns of data that may provide insight are columns such as "average order value" (number of items, cost), "Payment status" (this column lets you know if your payments have actually cleared and entered your account), "fulfillment status" (this column lets you know what stage of fulfillment a given order is undergoing) "Customer Name", and "Customer id." These last two columns are useful for keeping track of who orders when and can be used to offer loyal customers discounts or to keep track of orders for a loyalty program (see chapter five for more details), to make sure your customers keep coming back to reorder.

The "Average Order Value Over Time" report is very similar to the "Sales Over Time" report but with far fewer default columns in the summary beneath the graph. These columns are "hour," "total sales," "orders," and "average order value." You can, however, still customize this with as many columns as you would like, export, save, and print the report.

You can view these reports and any additional reports you have access to from the "Reports" tab. There are many different categories and reports available for business owners. These categories include sales, acquisition, retail sales, profit margin, customers, behavior, finances, marketing, and custom reports. You can choose to use as many or as few of these as you wish to keep track of your business and make key decisions for the future of your company.

Marketing
The marketing tab can be found on the navigation pane on the left-hand side of your screen, represented by a megaphone icon. It is from this tab that you can keep track of, start, or manage any campaigns and discounts you wish to run or are currently running. This tab will also keep track of the amount of money you have spent on marketing and the sales total for your company. From this tab, you can launch one of Shopify's pre-made marketing campaigns for your business or create your own marketing campaign. Some of these preset campaigns include campaigns for the holidays, Facebook ad campaigns, and even Google's ad services. These premade campaigns can be modified to fit your business, and customized to meet any budget, target demographic, or even location.

Once you have created a marketing campaign through Shopify, you can the software to use by adding activities to this campaign. Shopify currently only offers Facebook carousel ads, Facebook dynamic ads, and Google shopping campaigns by default, but more ad programs can be added manually using the apps tab, which will be discussed later.

Discounts

On the navigation pane, you will notice a tab labeled "Discounts," with two pages underneath it. This will be represented by a percentage sign within an ellipse. The two pages underneath the "Discounts" tab will be titled "Codes" and "Automatic." These are the two types of discounts you can create through your Shopify store.

For a discount code, you must first determine the code you want your customers to punch in to receive the discount. There are really two ways to generate discount codes. You can either name the code something relevant to the time of year or sale, such as "BacktoSchool," or you can click that handy dandy blue button in the top right of the discount code box labeled "Generate code," and Shopify will generate a random code for your customers to use. The second method is more secure but is less memorable to your customers, and vice versa. There are multiple types of discounts one can use through Shopify, labeled "Percentage," "Fixed amount," "Free shipping," and "Buy X Get Y." The title of each of these codes is self-explanatory as to their function. Each one of the aforementioned codes have requirements and variables that you can set for someone to meet to be eligible.

Note: Manual discount codes cannot be entered on orders that have an automatic discount code applied. This is largely in place to prevent someone from stacking a dozen discount codes and you losing money.

In addition to setting the requirements for the discount, and the value, you can set the minimum requirements for a code to be applicable, as well as who can use the code, and what items or collections it can be used on. You could set a policy of free shipping on orders of one hundred fifty dollars or more and enter that as a code (although that would be better off being used as an automatic discount). Regardless of who had the code, only those who met the minimum requirements would be able to apply the code at checkout. Being able to apply the code to specific groups is very useful if you wish to reward groups of customers, or your long-time customers, as you can group their profiles into the people who can use that code. You can also set usage limits for the codes, and the window of time for which it will work, to both the date and minute.

Automatic discounts are just as editable and customizable, but they do not require your customer to type in a code to use it. For example, if you set a free shipping policy on orders of one hundred fifty dollars or more, you could set the automatic discount to apply to anyone who checks out with one hundred and fifty dollars or more in their cart, without your customer ever having to keep track of and enter a code.

Apps

This tab will be located in the navigation pane on the left-hand side of the screen and represented by three squares arranged in a backward "L" shape, with an addition sign where the gap in the L is. This tab cannot be explained in as much detail as the other pages since doing so would mean that this section could be out of date by the time of publishing (due to the frequent addition or removal of apps from the Shopify store). But this page is where you can add apps to integrate external services with your business, whether Shopify sanctioned or not, by using the "Private apps" option. These apps can be coded to do anything that you either disagree with Shopify's methodology for or add any business specific features to your store.

The main page of this section will have suggested apps for your business, as well as a list of any currently installed applications you have. There will also be a "Visit the Shopify App Store" button, which will take you to Shopify's custom app store. In this store, apps can be found for a wide array of prices, both free and paid. If you have a specific app in mind, you can search using the search bar on their app store, or you can view apps by category if you only have a general idea of the type of application your business needs. Always make sure to double check the price to avoid unexpected charges to your

Chapter 2: Finding Products to Sell

In a world of so many products being made and sold, how do you know what items you should sell? This is the central question addressed in this chapter.

What to look at
When trying to determine what product to sell, ask yourself these three questions;

- What problem does this product solve?
- How many people deal with this problem (how large is the market)?
- What other products exist to solve this problem?

Often times, businesses buy products and they fail to sell. This is something that can easily be avoided if the product solves a problem that no other product does, one that is a massive problem. Some products even solve a problem that the consumer did not know they had until they saw the product.

As an example, we can look at the "Scrub Daddy." This product was featured on the Television Series "Shark Tank." As is demonstrated, this product acts as both a regular dish-washing tool, a cup cleaner, a spoon cleaner, and a tough scrubbing foam. All with different elements of the design, including "Flexfoam," a patented technology by the ScrubDaddy company. In 2018, this company was valued at over 170 million US Dollars! Who thought that a twist on the simple dish-washing market could be so successful?

That little yellow sponge is a great example of a pitch that solved a problem, the dilemma of spending so much money on four or five different tools to do what this one little sponge could do so much quicker. The market for this product was the majority of the world, most of the world washes some kind of dishes every day, and only a conglomeration of other products could work together to solve this problem. So, this product;

- Solved an inefficiency
- Had a worldwide market
- And no real competitors

It met the above criteria, and it took off by storm.

Additionally, you want to look at what your store will sell; you want to understand how a given product will fit in with other products you sell. For example, "Hot Topic," a fandom-based US store has products that all fit within its themes of "Pop Culture" merchandise. It has a select market and is a successful business. It Reported 174 million US dollars in sales in the first quarter of 2013

Chapter 3: Developing Your Inventory

Developing and maintaining your inventory is one of the most important factors in managing a successful store. The following chapter lays out some tips and answers for the following questions, "Should I reorder? When do I reorder? How much do I reorder? How do I keep track of my inventory more efficiently?" All of these questions will be answered in the following chapter.

Should you reorder

The first step when determining whether or not you should reorder a product is to look at how long your inventory has been sitting there, unsold. If Reba's office supplies have one thousand sets of a type of pen that have been sitting around for twelve months, she should probably terminate that product and even consider liquidating it (selling it for the cost you paid to prevent a loss). However, if a product has only been in storage for a few weeks and you are turning it over in a few weeks per order, you should reorder that product. If she has one thousand pens and she sells fifty sets daily on average, she should definitely re-order that supply.

The second step to determining whether or not to reorder a product is to consider how much of your profits it represents. This will also play a role in how many to reorder, and when to reorder. If a product represents any portion of your profits that covers more than the cost of the overhead to sell it, it should be reordered. Otherwise, it should be terminated.

When to Reorder

So, you have determined that you need to reorder a product, but when should you do that? A good idea is to base your reorder timetable off of the rate of sale and the shipping time for that particular product. Generally, you should order more when you have enough to last twice the maximum shipping time. For example, if Reba is ordering more copier paper, and she sells 10 boxes a day, with a four to seven-day shipping window, she should order more when she has 140 boxes left. This is largely, so you do not run out of a product, even if items get lost in shipping, poor weather delays the shipment, or an accident delays the shipment. This plans for the worst-case scenario and leaves you with inventory to spare. However, if you are running on a tighter budget or one with less space for inventory, you can order at one and a half times the maximum shipping time and still probably be ahead of the curve. It is unlikely that the shipping times will ever exceed one and a half times what they claim their maximum to be, but it still could happen. Another reason to order more when you hit one half of the supply you are going to self in the shipping window is in case there is a sudden uptick in the number of that particular item bought for whatever reason.

How much to Reorder

There are a few general principles for how much to reorder that one should follow. Largely the amount you should reorder depends on how fast it is selling and how long you have had it. If you have had a product for a long time and it reliable sells through quickly, you should order a fairly large quantity. However, if you just added a product and it is selling really quick, you should still be careful in your orders because it could very well just be a fad or a result of the new addition. Once you have had a product for about two months, that is generally long enough to gauge whether it is a fad. As a rule of thumb, your order for an item should rarely, if ever, exceed 133% percent of your last order, and shouldn't often exceed 120%. This minimizes the risk, as if your last order sold through quickly, an order of the same size should do the same, presuming there isn't a finite nature to the market and that the sales have remained consistent. The additional thirty-three percent allows you to expand to meet higher demand without winding up wasting a lot of money on something that will not sell. If you are a bigger company, you can afford to take a risk, but for smaller businesses especially, I urge you to stick to these guidelines.

Keeping track of inventory

Keeping track of your inventory is important for many reasons, the first and foremost being so that you do not sell out of an item, that makes up a large portion of your revenue, and lost out on a lot of sales and revenue because of it. There are lots of different software applications that can log inventory for you, but I recommend Shopify's for ease of use and reliability. It is always a good idea to do a physical inventory check periodically to make sure nothing is amiss with your digital ledger. Stay on top on sales rates, inventory stock, and reorders, and you should be in good shape.

Chapter 4: Finding Customers

This is where most businesses struggle, finding the consumer that needs their product. The first step to success in this realm is to determine your target group. This makes advertising significantly easier; if you know your target demographic, you can then go about finding where they tend to spend their time. The central goal of finding a customer is simple; get the customer to your store or webpage and let your products speak for themselves. If you successfully choose a product based on Chapter 2's guidelines, you should have no problem selling it once you get the target demographic into the store or on the web page.

But how do you figure out your target demographic? That can be a complex question, but usually, a small line of logic and perhaps some data-gathering can lead you to your target demographic. The first question to ask yourself is "what is the use of this product?" once you determine the use you can then ask, "who would use this/who would use this the most?" if you are unsure, here is where surveys can come in handy. You can conduct a survey (online surveys are probably the most effective for an online business, and in person surveys are probably the most effective for a brick and mortar store). The survey should ask very direct questions about the product and if the people face the problem that the product solves. Then you analyze the data and determine what group responded affirmatively to the question about facing the problem. From there, you can ask around and try to determine where that demographic spends their time (either digitally or a physical place) and advertise appropriately.

That is the second step of any customer acquisition, making sure the customer knows you exist. The greatest strategies for finding most demographics is simple, social media. Most countries have large social media presence, while some countries place heavy restrictions on social media. There are a few routes one can take with this approach. Firstly, creating a corporate account is a necessity on most of these platforms, and do not forget to add a link to your store on the profile! Alternatively, you can pay to put advertisements in front of your demographic on these sites. You can pay to advertise on Facebook, YouTube, Tik Tok, Instagram, or even Tumblr. For more details on advertising specific strategies, see chapter 9.

One way to capitalize on your already existing customers is to offer a discount code to users who refer to other people. Offering a one-time use discount codes or credit to users who refer others is a relatively popular strategy, employed by huge businesses, such as Wish.com and Tesla Motors. The way this works is when someone buys their first product, they enter the username of the person who referred them, and that user gets a discount code or store credit assigned to their account. This encourages users to advertise for you, online and to their friends. Word of mouth is a great way to market your business, and even better when it is supplemented by extra incentive.

Another great opportunity to attract new customers is to advertise for a massive sale that you are about to begin, as people get curious about sales and are likely to go to the location just to "check out the offerings."

There are many services that have software for purchase so that you can use to send out emails to a broad range of people (such as icontact). These emails, while they often get filled under spam, will reach some people, and if composed correctly, they will reach your demographic and boost your sales.

Setting up a booth at an event for people who could use your product would be a great way to acquire new customers, with very little cost! For example, if you sell clothes and garments, you might want to set up at your location fashion convention to reach many people interested in your product in one day. If you are selling musical instruments, you should consider setting up at a musical event in a big city near you.

Additionally, speaking out for values you align your business with can attract new customers. However, this tactic can spark backlash and start some groups boycotting your business. This can get you a large amount of publicity, and the people who support what you stand for will often flock to your business, even if it isn't located somewhere they might normally go. Aligning your business with one set of values or another is a risky business for brick and mortar stores. It can also be risky for online retailers, but generally, they face less risk using this tactic. Speaking out for values you stand for, while risky, can pay off in a big way if successful. Advocating for these values at conventions, to your congressmen, and at any public event give you publicity, which is what drives people to your store. Becoming an ally of a group of people makes them more likely to spend their money at your store rather than your opponents; after all, we all want to support the causes we believe in any way we realistically can.

Considering a strategic partnership can also bring many benefits to the table. If you are producing medicine that suppresses withdrawl symptoms for alcohol, you may well want to partner with an organization like Alcoholics Anonymous or others. If you have a better way to can sodas, you should approach Coca-Cola or another large producer of caffeinated beverages. Any ally you have in your market can provide valuable assets; you just have to find an ally who has a product or service that compliments your product or service.

Chapter 5: Sustaining Customers Long Term

Sustaining customers is all about making your customer feel valued. It is all about making *their* lives easier and better. Have you ever ordered a product offline, only to be horribly disappointed when it arrived? I know I have, and it is even more frustrating when the company will not take ownership for their mistake and refund your money. That is an excellent example of what *not* to do. Remember the saying "The Customer is always right," and live by it.

First, having an excellent return policy is a good idea. If you have a costumer who is dissatisfied by their product and tries to take it back in a short timeframe, give them a refund. Be upfront about your return policy and make the process easy for the customer. You will make them more likely to return a product they do not like, but that just means they're back on your site, and if the process is easy for them, they are much more likely to return and purchase another item. Amazon has great success with this policy; Amazon returns are painless, quick, and convenient for the customer (or at least as convenient as a return can be). This makes it much more likely for a consumer to buy from them if they know that "If I do not like this, I'll just return it." Offer a refund in cash or store credit. If you offer store credit, tack on a little extra to make it more tempting. If they choose the store credit option, remember that you are not really losing that sale, just postponing it at worst. Choosing the credit option means that they either have to come back to your site and spend the money (only costing you the wholesale as opposed to the cash value of the product), or they never spend it, and it is like they never even returned the product.

Return your customer's communications. This includes calls, texts, emails, and whatever other sources you have communication through. In this aspect, time is of the essence. Remember to be polite in these communications, and most importantly, helpful. Set expectations in your voice mail and meet them. Do not say that you will call them back in the next two business days and then call them on the third day. Say you will call them within two business days and call them back the very next business day. Go above and beyond what you promise your customers. Also, make clear your policies on things like returns, no receipt returns, your loyalty program, gift cards, store credit, and any other aspect of your business that isn't treated the same universally.

If you make a mistake, not only correct it but overcorrect it. This often makes your customer less upset with you, and an unexpected gift can go a long way to establish trust in a business relationship. An easy and low-cost way for you to do this is to give them something, like a coupon. A 10% coupon will often do the trick, it makes your consumer happier, and the sale they use that coupon on will likely still be profitable. Additionally, you will have just earned a new customer. Alternatively, you could use a gift card to your store. Another option for making your customer happy when correcting their order is to give them a smaller item, or even a collection of items, from your store for free with their order.

A great way to keep customers once you have them is by creating a loyalty system. The overall goal of this system is to reward the customers for returning and buying your product, and there are several ways to do this. First, you should use a tiered system, with the different steps being labeled with different, distinctly positive traits. Usually, a four-tier system works well, beginning with those who rarely buy from your store, and gradually increasing until you have people who use your store often. Second, the reward should get better and better with each tier, adding on rewards at each tier. Third, you should add a really big reward to the final tier, as they will have had to have been a loyal customer to achieve that tier. Fourth, you should reset this system annually, to prevent losses and increase the incentive to order regularly. Fifth, it is highly recommended that you give acknowledgment and thanks to those who reach the final tier and ask if they would like to have their name published as a top tier patron on your website.

Below is an example of a tiered loyalty system (as described above) for "Reba's Office," which is a fictional, online office supply store.

New Patron: tier one customer

Requirements: Make one purchase (of ten dollars or more) within the year

Rewards: Get a ten percent discount on your second order of the year

Title: Humble Patron; Tier two customer

Requirements: Make ten or more purchases (of ten dollars or more) in a year

Rewards: five percent discount on ALL orders for your one-year status, one entry in a drawing to win thirty-five dollars in store credit, every additional purchase grants an additional entry.

Title: Kind Patron; tier three customer

Requirements: Make twenty-five or more purchases (of ten dollars or more) in a year

Rewards: A seven and a half percent discount on ALL orders for the next year, five additional entries into the drawing for thirty-five dollars store credit,

One entry into the drawing for seventy dollars store credit, with every additional purchase giving you another ticket

Earn fifteen dollars store credit anytime you place an order of one hundred dollars or more (before shipping)

Title: Reliable Patron

Requirements: Make Fifty or more purchases (of ten dollars or more) within the year

Rewards: ten percent discount on all purchases for one year

Twenty entrances into the drawing for thirty-five dollars store credit

Ten entrances in the drawing for seventy dollars store credit

Free Shipping on all orders over ten dollars for a year

Your name on the Website banner

Anytime you spend one hundred fifty dollars or more, earn thirty dollars store credit

All Drawings will occur once every three months and be done live on our YouTube channel, "Reba's office supplies 19"

A handwritten thank you letter

One of the biggest things you can do to sustain long term customers is incredibly simple, listen to any feedback they give you. Make sure to thank them for the feedback. When you are first starting, I would ever take the time to hand write thank you cards to those who provide constructive criticism of your business.

Make sure to take their suggestions into consideration. Feedback is key to improving your business. Sometimes you should even initiate feedback by asking them to take a quick survey once they have purchased something or spent a certain amount of time on your site.

One more important act you can use; be credible. Deliver on your promises, and if things change, let people know up front. Try to deliver even more than you promise. If you say a product will be launched at a specific date, launch it on that day, or do everything in your power to. Establishing trust is very important for a consumer base.

Chapter 6: Let's Get Competitive

Competition can be a problem for any business, but especially for smaller businesses. Luckily, there are many ways to beat out the competition.

Ask your customers for feedback and listen to their feedback. If there is something they do not like, change it. If there is something they want to see happen, put time, effort, and resources towards making it happen. Your customers are your lifeline in business, please them, and they will reward you. See what the customer likes about your competition and see if you can do more of that. Remember, a lot of businesses do not really listen to their feedback as much as they should. Exploit that chink in the armor, be the one who listens and that is an immediate advantage over many of your competitors. If you show your customer you care, they are much more likely to give their loyalty to you.

Test your product at different price points. See how well it sells at all price points where you are making money. Analyze the profits for a different price point and sales. A great way to do this is to run a holiday sale. This way, your customers will not be annoyed by the changing prices, and make sure it is clear that it is a sale. Then, if that price worked significantly better, try running it at that price for a week or so after some time has passed. If you like the margins there and they work, keep them that way. Even when you have found the right price to sell your product at, run sales periodically. Make sure not to sell the products for less than you pay for them, but still tack a 5-25% off discount a few times a year. Even though these sales may seem to hurt your profits significantly, advertise them so that you can attract new customers. Often times, if people see that there is a big sale going on somewhere (whether digital or physical), they are more likely to go check out the store. Remember that pricing is one of the major keys of running a successful business. If the price isn't right, the customer simply will not bite.

An easy thing that you can even do through Shopify is giving out coupons/discount codes. Send them through email, physical mail, text, or any other print delivery method. Just make sure to send them to customers who either already have purchased multiple times or are first time customers. Another tactic employed by many companies is to give someone a big discount (like 40%) on their first purchase, often in leu of advertising. This way the cost of acquisition is minimal, so long as you do not let the discount cut past the wholesale cost.

Keep track of the market. Pay attention to customer behavior, what works, what does not work, and how people respond to changes (or lack of changes). Several of the tools on Shopify are meant to do this. There is a whole category of data reporting tools dedicated to customer behavior and habits if you pay for a higher plan; these tools can be vital to your business. If you notice the market has shifted away from an item and is no longer buying it, stop selling it. You must pay attention to the market if you wish to be successful, being blind to shifts in the market can bring down the tallest of giants in the business world. Think about Sears Holding Corporation, they were dominating the hardware industry in 2007, but now they are going bankrupt. They failed to stay atop the market. They failed to pay attention to trends and did not adjust to shifts. That's why they went from having a value of over $130 dollars a share to the less than $1 share value they have now. That is a massive loss and is a strong example of why paying attention to the market is critically important in business. So, make sure to pay attention to what the market demands. The larger of a company you become, the greater importance this will hold.

Acquire new products. If you are noticing that there is a really popular item your competition is selling, begin selling it. If you see a product explode overnight, buy it, but be cautious. Do not do massive orders, for that could leave you sitting on losses when that fad dies. Buy relatively small orders and watch the sell-through rate.

Improve your customer service. There is always room for improvement here, and your business will be no exception. Always strive to provide the best experience for your customers. If people will be spending large amounts of time at your store, or you want to keep them in the store longer, add beverages to your items. Maybe even have free water (fountain or tap, not bottled), but do not charge ridiculous prices for drinks. Take a little bit of margin on them, but do not overcharge or bet on them being a large portion of your money. If you have a book store, add some couches so people can sit down and read a few pages to know if they want the book. If you have a video game shop, have some demos and some seating. Let your customer try the product, and often they will be more willing to buy it.

Add a bulk discount, say you spend $150, you get $15 in gift card, or off your order. That can push people that little extra way to get them to spend some more. Add value to spending more. Send follow up emails when a product gets delivered, asking if it was as described on your site, or if there are any more details that should be added to the product page. Make your customer feel that they matter and that they have input, and they will come back.

Chapter 7: Finding New Products

Expanding your product line is an important part of growing and business, whether it be in a traditional store or an online retailer. There are many ways to go about this, and some are more viable than others for some businesses. Attending trade shows, spending time in online forums, surveys, innovating, and visiting your competitor are all great ways to find new products. Always make sure to start with small orders to test your market for their receptiveness to these new items without getting burned.

Trade Shows

Trade shows are a great resource for anyone looking to expand their product line up, as that is what trade shows are all about. You may have to travel to get to a relevant trade show, but for most businesses, there is likely a relevant trade show that they can attend. After all, trade shows are where people take their products to debut, and there is no better way to stay on the bleeding edge of the market than snapping up products as soon as they are released. Just be careful to not get overexcited for a product by the sales pitch and to think critically about how this product would fit into your business.

Forums

Online forums are great places for digital retailers to not only advertise but also to get ideas for products to pick up. Often times forums will have someone asking where they can get a product, and what better way to find a customer than to address their needs directly? Also, places like amazon.com can show you valuable products, and their reviews are often very revealing about a range of products available from various distributors and manufacturers

Surveys

Surveys of your current clientele are likely the lowest risk way to add products to your line up. These surveys will often reveal what your current clientele actually want, regardless of what any big-name brands have to say. Remember to leave questions anonymous and open-ended. "Would you like to see more products in Reba's office supplies: yes or no," is a bad question. If they answer yes, congratulations, you have learned that they're not happy with their current lineup? But what now? If you use the above question, you have no idea how to improve. However, if you ask a question like "What additional products would you like to see at Reba's office supply store that you did not see today? (Note: your responses will be anonymized and kept that way). This question is better because you know there is something everyone wants to see at your store but asking them to answer directly means they are more likely to give you an honest answer. This way, you now also know how to fix their unhappiness, you now know what product they want to see.

Visiting your Competitor

A visit to your competitor on a busy day for them can be quite revealing, as you can see what items that they have which people are buying that you do not. You can also ask some of their customers what they think about your business, and most probably will not recognize you. This not only allows you to get a better understanding of what items to stock but also guidelines on how to improve your business.

Innovating

There is always room for you to create a product for your shelves only but remember when you are starting to work on that invention, make sure to ask yourself what problem it solves, who can use it and what other products exist to fill this role. Also remember that you can't get sentimental about an item, as money does not care if you are sentimental to an item. Not everything is a problem, and not everything has a solution.

Chapter 8: Make It Grow

Once your business is up and running steadily, how do you make it grow? This is the question this chapter seeks to address. There are many ways to make your business grow, but in the following pages what I believe to be the best strategies for business growth are documented.

There are three fundamental aspects to expanding your business, and the emphasis largely depends on whether or not you are an online business. The fundamental aspects are as follows, expanding your locations, spreading awareness, and product acquisition/ product termination. The first of these three aspects is not applicable to a strictly online retailer. It is, however, very important for a physical retailer.

Adding stores

There is only so much business and so many sales that can be conducted from one location, so as your business grows, you should seek to expand physical locations. There are two routes for doing this, franchising and opening more corporate stores. The first of these routes require less work on your part but offers less profit and less risk. The second of the routes offer the potential for more profit but requires significantly more work and offers significantly more risk. Before you add another store, it is highly recommended that you set up a website and stabilize that. This isn't a necessity for some businesses, but it is for most.

Franchising

Franchising is when you allow other people to use your branding, any patents and/or copyrights you own in exchange for them taking on all the risk and giving you a percentage of their profits, as well as an initial fee. A typical franchise deal might be structured as follows; you give them the rights to your products, services, and brand(s). They follow the rules and policies set by you, and they pay for the initial store construction as well as any other costs in setting it up. They give you an initial fee, and a percentage of their profits or sales, (often around the five to twelve percent mark). They are allowed to operate for a few decades typically, but it can be any length you determine, as long as they do not violate the terms of the contract, and they often set up a corporate sales account so that you (the corporate entity) can make sure you are being paid correctly. They handle the day to day operations of the business, and receive the significant majority share of the profits, and take on the risk, but they get access to your brand and all associated entities. This works well for many incredibly large corporations, such as "McDonald's" and "Taco Bell."

The cost of setting up the initial franchise is typically hundreds of thousands of dollars. For example, the McDonalds website says that it requires one to have at least five hundred thousand dollars in liquid assets available. Additionally, they are required to attend special training, according to their site, this lasts for between twelve and eighteen months. There is a lot of flexibility you can have when setting the requirements for franchising, but your first couple stores should only be franchised when you are doing amazing, and when you are confident the market can support more stores. The first several franchises will be individual negotiations, and likely have different terms, that is okay. As long as you are comfortable with the conditions upon which both franchises are built, the terms are okay. It is also advisable to err on the side of caution with these terms. If you are not comfortable at the rate they offer, make them meet you or simply pass on their offer. Sometimes deals aren't meant to be. Sometimes it will not happen. Franchising is about building a network, you have to trust the people you franchise to because they also speak for your brand.

Corporate Stores

An alternative to franchising, corporate stores mean you take all the risk and all the reward. This is similar to setting up your original shop, except this time you do not have to build your brand all over again. You still have to either lease or build a space, order the supplies, and get your network setup, but you do not have to worry as much about building the brand. You take the risk as if the store fails, you will literally pay for it. On the flip side of that coin, if it succeeds all the profits go to you. One of the most important aspects of corporate stores is to hire a manager you trust.

This manager will be responsible for the day to day operations when you are not there. That means they could very well be the factor that makes or breaks your second location. Having a manager, you can trust to run the show when you aren't there is key, because you simply cannot be at all your stores at once. It isn't physically possible. Make sure you are confident in your pick for manager, and make sure to give them extra training. Something to beat into their head is simple; "When in doubt, contact us!" if your manager has their doubts about a course of action, they should contact the owner(s). If they make a massive mistake on an important decision, they could sink that store, it is a lot of trust to put in one person.

You will have to be involved in the construction negotiations and set up of at least the first few corporate stores. Even if you did not, you should be. This experience could prove an invaluable asset down the line when someone comes to you with questions about a new store. Remember, experience is paramount in business. If you do not have it, either get it or find someone who has experience. Err on the side of caution when unsure but trust your instincts generally.

Product Acquisition and Termination
There are many ways to acquire a product, but those will be discussed in depth in chapter 7. Acquiring new products is a vital part of any business' expansion, and

there is much that should go into each decision. Terminating products is another vital part of any successful business, but it isn't talked about nearly as much, despite its necessity. It is undoubtedly an unpleasant part of business, telling someone that their product did not make the cut, but business is adapt or die in the modern age.

Acquisition:

When to acquire new products is a difficult and intimidating decision. Wasting money can destroy a business, so it is always a decision that should require substantial thought. To get more people into your store, one way is to expand your product categories or to add more products to an existing category. These are powerful tools, but dangerous ones. When your business is flourishing but stable, one should acquire new products. Making the decision, too should be done carefully and discussed thoroughly. You should likely talk to an expert if you are considering adding a product, and you should always be willing to listen to their advice. Make sure to analyze your market data and trends.

So, you have decided to add a product. But what product do you add? How will it impact the sales of your other products? These are all important questions to ask yourself. Each question will have a distinct answer for each business that it is being asked about, as well as each time you add a product to your line up. As for what product to add, you should consider whether you want to expand on an already present type of item in your store or add an entirely new type of item. An example of expanding on an already present type of item would be adding another pen to the line up of pens at Reba's Office supply store. An example of adding an entirely new item would be like adding sticker paper to your crafts items.

If you add to an existing item type's selection (such as a new pen), you may detract from the sales of some of your other pens, but you also may be making more money off of the new pens. You would likely also attract new customers who are loyal to that specific type of pen (yes, pen loyalists exist). This is a trade-off that should be weighed carefully. Often times clicking around on online forums and reviews of products may reveal the quality of a product and the public opinion on the product without you having to risk your money on it.

On the other hand, if you add a new category, you risk it not selling. If you perform surveys to determine what product to add, that will greatly lessen the chance of a complete failure, but the product may not perform spectacularly. You are more likely to attract new customers this way, as you expand the potential uses for the products in your store. It is a trade-off worth considering, and if you are getting multiple requests for a specific item, it is often best to buy a small quantity and test the sell-through rate (see chapter 7 for more information). Even if it remains a small loss, you have pleased some of your customers, which increases their chances of returning to your store and buying more items, so all is not lost.

Terminating an item:

Terminating an item can be a very unpleasant decision, as you will likely upset some of your customers, but it is a decision that must be done rationally and without empathy. Look at your sales reports, how much of your sales is a certain product? How fast does it turn over? How much of your total business' shelf space is this product taking up? All of these questions should be considered when decided if/ when to terminate a product or service from your line of offerings.

If a product is turning over (i.e., selling) really fast right now, you probably will not want to terminate it, even if it is only a small portion of your sales because it is serving a really important role; getting people into your store. Once they're in your store, it is much more likely that they will buy something else.

If an item is taking up a large portion of your shelf space, whether that be on display or on storage, it should be considered for trimming. This does not mean cut it entirely, but if you are ordering large quantities only for them to sit around for a long time, try to trim back how many you are ordering, and trim down the number on the shelves. This makes room for other products, products which will likely make you more money.

If an item is barely accounting for any profits, it should likely be cut. This likely means it isn't selling well (or at the right price) and isn't worth the time, effort, or capitol to continue selling. No doubt cutting a product will upset some of your customers, but it gives you more space for your better products, and the may bulk order right before it is removed if you advertise it well and they actually care.

Spreading Awareness
Many times, the problem with growing a business is simply that people are unaware of this business' existence. There are many ways to do "traditional" advertising, but those will be covered in chapter nine. Below is a list of other potential ways to spread awareness of your business, without spending a ton on advertising.

Firstly, attend any networking events you can. These can be conventions of your demographics, to product-fares, to leadership training. Attending networking events can get you connections to others in your market or a complimentary market. Another great idea to draw attention to your business is to invite bloggers and reporters to sit down with you and do an interview, or to review your business. This way, you both benefit, you give them content to write about and you get advertisement.

Advocating for values you believe in, as well as speaking out for those causes can get you news coverage and a widely recognizable brand name. Encouraging society to be responsible for its shortcoming and discriminatory policies is a great place to begin your public appearance. Another great topic, to begin with, is making corporations take responsibility for their impacts and responsibilities to society at large. For example, a corporation should not discriminate against any group of people, even if it is profitable for them. As another example, if a company knows nicotine is bad for you and can kill you, they shouldn't keep producing nicotine-based products, and they should certainly stop developing new nicotine products that feature a higher concentration(s) of nicotine.

Chapter 9: Marketing Your Business

In the modern world, how do you market your business? In a world of instant searches and dying in print articles, do you go all digital, all print, or a mixture? If you go digital, what style of marketing do you use?

There are many ways to market one's business, and it there isn't a one size fits all solution. Luckily, this guide will cover all that you need to know in the modern age, and guide you through determining your best marketing solution, and what all of the jargon means. Some of the most worthwhile marketing ventures are as follows; influencers, charity donations, giving seminars and free classes, digital advertisements with a pay per click structure, business alliances, and referral rewards.

Determining what marketing method works best for your business

Each business has its own set of assets, resources, values, and target demographic. This is largely the reason that there isn't a one size fits all marketing solution. But that's okay; each demographic will be easier to reach using certain methods. First, you have to determine your target demographic (see chapter four for a guide on how to do that), then you need to find out how to best get a hold of them. Public surveys often work best; if you're looking for a younger demographic, often times you can piece together how to find them simply by spending some time on the internet.

For middle-aged and older demographics, you may want to use newspaper advertising or Facebook advertising. When in doubt, looking at the Facebook and YouTube usage demographics can give you valuable insight into where you might find your demographic. Both are massive giants in the entertainment world, and you can advertise for much cheaper on those platforms than you would be able to say on, television ad space, some of the most expensive ad space in the world.

This is where your resources come into play. If you have mountains of cash, you might use television ad space, as it reaches far more people and demographics than any other method in the shortest amount of time, but it costs the most. If you're in doubt of what to advertising method to use, you can often conduct surveys or look at published usage data for big websites. As traditional television dies, perhaps you should use Google's ad sense, a service which uses bidding takes into account your click-through rate, your payment, and your budget to find relevant customers. But more on that below. Essentially, finding your method will take time, effort, resources, and experimentation. Once you have found your target demographic, both in the deterministic and literal sense, you can choose a marketing strategy.

Giving to charity

Giving to charity can help your business in several ways. Firstly, there are massive tax deductions for giving to recognized non-profit institutions. Second, making a big money donation can get your business a lot of press coverage, spreading the word about your business. In addition, people are more willing to spend money if they know that a portion of it is going to a good cause. If you see a headline in the news about a local business donating ten thousand dollars to let's say, the Saint Jude's children hospital, you will remember that when you see their name. Are you more likely to check out their website, or the site of some competitor who used that money to buy space on your Facebook feed? I know I would rather check out and support a business that is saving lives. To that end, pledging to give a small portion of all your profits (for instance, five percent) to a charity is a great way to get press, tax deductions, and support a good cause. Perhaps an even better way to get that press is to set up a system where each year you give five percent (or whatever percentage of profits you choose) to a different charity. This would get you press each year, a sizable tax deduction, and you would be helping a good cause. This strategy works even better if you are a proud advocate for the type of issues that you are donating towards fixing.

Influencers

Influencers are a great way to target specific demographics. For instance, if you are trying to sell a better gaming mouse, you may want to sponsor a youtuber like Markiplier, PewDiePie, or JackSepticEye. These people largely do video game videos and will get millions of views per video. Getting one of these people to endorse your product can get your business hundreds or even thousands of new customers from one video. You may even consider sponsoring multiple videos. Another great way to tie Influencers and Charity Donations together is to find a youtuber who does charity live streams (such as Markiplier) and make a big money donation during the stream. Then you will be able to use this as a platform to get the youtuber to endorse your business and get their viewers curious. But make sure to talk to the streamer beforehand and plan it out, so you get the response you need!

Business Alliances

Another great way to get marketing is by forming a business alliance with a business that you will both benefit from. If you have a real estate business and forge a business alliance with a furniture company, you can refer each other customers. Often times, people are looking for furniture before they consider moving, and that is the type of referral that can be beneficial for both parties. People almost always buy new furniture after they move and getting a small discount because of a referral can encourage customers to go to you over your competitors.

Speakers, seminars

A great way to get people into your store if you are a traditional retailer is by inviting speakers to come to your business and speak with locals about issues that may hit close to home. There are many speakers who could come speak about many different issues, all of which will depend on your city and your clientele. Remember, getting people in the door is ninety percent of the battle when it comes to sales.

Traditional Advertisements

There are many different methods of sales that fall under this category. In this section, we will cover two of the most effective methods for advertisements, regardless of your status as either a physical or digital retailer. Largely we will determine efficacy by the cost per customer acquisition. The strategies we will cover are the digital Pay per Click structure of advertisements, and the Pay Per View model.

Pay per click

Pay Per Click (PPC) is one of the most used models of advertising when it comes to digital advertising. In this model you pay a platform, for example, Google, to put the advertisement you construct for them in front of their users, and you pay them every time someone clicks on your ad, which will lead that person to your website. The price is negotiated up front, and some companies will let you set an upper limit on the total amount paid to them for your ad. Every click will cost you a number of cents (usually), and a typical number would be a price between twenty-five and fifty cents per click. The lower you can get the price per click. Obviously the better off you will be.

A key to successfully deploying this strategy is to know how many visitors go to your site (on average) before any purchase is made. This will give you an idea of what price you should be willing to pay when combined with the average profit off of a sale. As an example, let us say that Reba's office supply store is advertising through the Google Search Engine. From looking at the traffic metrics provided by her Advanced Shopify plan, she knows that every fiftieth costumer (on average) buys a set of her premium pens, and an artisan leather-bound notebook which is listed at a price that brings her a profit of Fifty-five dollars. Now, a general rule of thumb is that you should not pay more than a third of your profits to advertisement. Now, if we divide her profits (fifty-five dollars) by her number of customers to achieve said profits (fifty), then we get one dollar and ten cents per customer. If we wish to obey the one-third rule of thumb, we then divide the dollar and ten cents by three, which yields thirty-six point six cents as the maximum amount she should pay per click.

Now, the smaller the website, typically the more negotiable the pricing is, at the cost of getting fewer clicks, so it is a tradeoff. If you are seeking ads from a larger business, they tend to be less negotiable on pricing, as they have multiple people fighting for that slot. However, this allows for significantly faster growth of your business. If you go with a smaller website, you will have more negotiation room and likely higher profit margins, but this will come at the cost of the speed of growth of your business.

Pay Per View Model

This is another really effective advertisement strategy, regardless of your status as an online or physical retailer. Much like the pay per click model, the negotiations will depend on the company, content of the ad, and the relationship to the business. However, this model is less efficient if you have a lower quality ad banner. If you have a great marketing team and great advertisements, this can be a valid option. With this structure you will typically be paying between one and two dollars for every thousand people who view your ad. If your ad is very attention-getting grabbing and effective in getting someone to click to your website, then this is likely a better strategy for your business.

Chapter 10: Reinvesting in Your Store

Knowing when and how much to invest can be the difference between a $10,000 business and a $10,000,000 business, as reinvestment fuels growth. In most industries, it is estimated that you should reinvest between 25% and 50% of profits when focusing on company growth. There are three basic categories this reinvestment should go towards are, freeing up time, professional development, and expansion.

Freeing up time

Part of the capitol investment should go towards freeing up your time and your manager's time. This can include hiring a professional bookkeeper, hiring a dedicated training person, and putting more personnel onto the public relations and customer service teams. Freeing up your time and the time of higher-level management allows for professional development, which will improve performance drastically.

Professional Development

Now that you have more time on the hands of yourself and upper management, it is time for some professional development. What do you mean by professional development, you may ask? Going to business training seminars, management seminars, public relations seminars, or any kind of training designed to help you in the business world is professional development. You can also use this time to network, going to product fares, high-level business discussions, or even use the time to consult a business coach or mentor. This can be especially useful for your first company, as there are some things that experience triumphs all in, such as termination and acquisition decisions.

Expansion
When reinvesting, this is where the largest portion of capitol should go. There is a much more in-depth review of general guidelines for growing your business in chapter 8, but this list focusses on expansions every business can do, while the former simply give ideas for businesses that may not be applicable to every business.

One important part of the expansion is understanding the experience your customers have and knowing any pain-points they may have in dealing with your business. This part of the equation is best solved using "mystery shoppers," people you pay to buy from your business, go through customer support phone calls, etc. and have them report back to you so that you know how your regular service is. The idea between not just doing it yourself is that you may be recognized, and they may give you preferential treatment. The larger you grow, the more important doing this is, as the greater a quantity you expand to, the harder it is to monitor quality. Once you have these reports, they give you knowledge that can tell you where you need to invest. Was checkout really slow? Invest in better equipment and infrastructure.

Was customer support rude and unhelpful, train customer support and if it continues, fire troublemakers. Was your store complicatedly organized so that it was difficult and frustrating to find products? Streamline the organization of your store. Was the fastest shipping option too slow on a product? Start working out shipping options with international shipping companies (which Shopify does for you on the more expensive plans). Were they on hold for thirty minutes trying to contact customer support? Hire more staff to man phones. The point of a mystery shopper is that their reports give you ideas of the problems your company faces, and the hurtles your customers must go through. Once you know about these problems and hurdles, knowing what to fix is a lot clearer.

One major reinvestment you can make in your business is to buy another company and merge your two companies. This often requires millions or even billions of dollars, but better than bankrupting your competition, it adds their value, customers, and experience to your company, as well as their product portfolio. It does not have to be competitors that you buy, any business that fits your portfolio, expertise, and is profitable (and set to remain so) is likely a good purchase, but you should always consult an expert and get multiple opinions on this matter, as these matters are some of the most complicated maneuvers you will ever make in the business world. Be careful to stay within the legal guidelines for avoiding monopolies or any other infractions that could occur from a merger. This maneuver, while complicated, can seriously boost your business to the top of the market, sometimes even doubling or tripling your revenue.

A reinvestment worth making is likely hiring a lawyer if you are above a few employees and/or locations. Or if you do not hire a lawyer, work out a deal with a law firm so that you have a lawyer on standby should something happen. Because there is a good chance that regardless of the ethicality with which you run your business, legal trouble will happen eventually, and it is better to have your legalism sorted out before you need it. Additionally, you should shop around for the best internet, phone, and any other service providers to try and trim cost while boosting performance.

Upgrading infrastructure is often also a valuable reinvestment. For an online retailer, this may include better computers and or servers to handle traffic smoothly or to store data for longer, or even to create redundancy in case something happens to your main system. There are many ways to upgrade your infrastructure for a digital marketplace, from new hard drives to switching to solid state drives, to upgrading to a RAID array or even just replacing that old desktop with a shiner, more powerful one.

For a physical business, you can upgrade your website with the above suggestions, and upgrade your physical stores. You can remodel them, giving your stores a newer, more polished look. Additionally, you can increase the lighting or the internet, you can add business phones, create another division responsible for location and franchise acquisition, give your workers more effective computers, upgrade your Shopify plan, or even open another corporate store.

Made in the USA
Columbia, SC
27 September 2019